2003

To: B

Merry Christmas!

Happy - oh - Happy

New Year!

Much Love

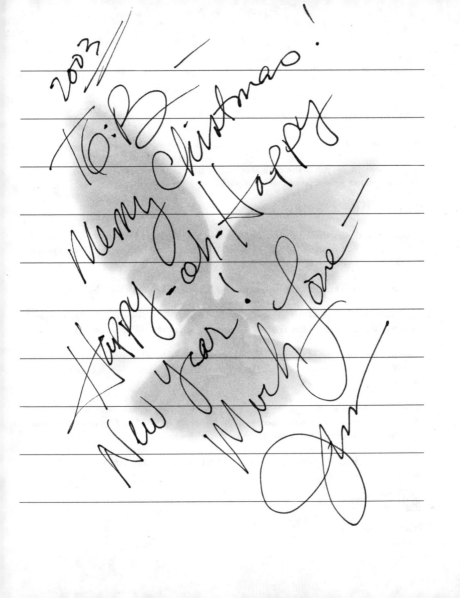

Cover image © GettyOne

Scripture quotations, unless otherwise noted, are taken from the HOLY BIBLE, NEW INTERNATIONAL VERSION®. NIV®. Copyright © 1973, 1978, 1984 by International Bible Society. Used by permission of Zondervan Publishing House. All rights reserved.

Scripture quotations marked KJV are taken from the King James Version of the Bible.

Scripture quotations marked TLB are taken from *The Living Bible* copyright © 1971. Used by permission of Tyndale House Publishers, Inc., Wheaton, Illinois 60189. All rights reserved.

Scripture quotations marked NLT are taken from the *Holy Bible,* New Living Translation, copyright © 1996. Used by permission of Tyndale House Publishers, Inc. Wheaton, Illinois 60189, U.S.A. All rights reserved.

Scripture quotations marked NRSV are taken from the New Revised Standard Version Bible, copyright 1989, Division of Christian Education of the National Council of the Churches of Christ in the United States of America. Used by permission. All rights reserved.

Published by Barbour Publishing, Inc., P.O. Box 719, Uhrichsville, Ohio 44683, www.barbourbooks.com

Member of the
Evangelical Christian
Publishers Association

Printed in China.
5 4 3 2 1

Let There Be

PEACE

on Earth

Larissa Nygren

DayMaker
GREETING BOOKS

THE
PRINCE OF PEACE
IS BORN

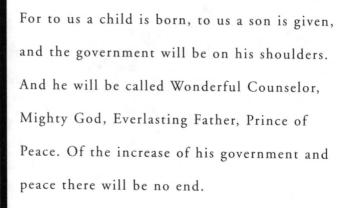

For to us a child is born, to us a son is given, and the government will be on his shoulders. And he will be called Wonderful Counselor, Mighty God, Everlasting Father, Prince of Peace. Of the increase of his government and peace there will be no end.

ISAIAH 9:6–7

And the angel said unto them, Fear not: for, behold,

I bring you good tidings of great joy,

which shall be to all people. For unto you is born this day

in the city of David a Saviour, which is Christ the Lord.

And this shall be a sign unto you; Ye shall find the babe

wrapped in swaddling clothes, lying in a manger.

And suddenly there was with the angel a multitude

of the heavenly host praising God, and saying,

Glory to God in the highest, and on earth peace,

good will toward men.

LUKE 2:10–14 KJV

COME WORSHIP
THE KING!
THE CHRIST CHILD
IS BORN!

He brought peace on earth
and wants to bring it also into your soul—
that peace which the world cannot give.
He is the One who would save His people from their sins.

CORRIE TEN BOOM

For God was pleased to have all his fullness dwell in him, and through him to reconcile to himself all things, whether things on earth or things in heaven, by making peace through his blood, shed on the cross.

COLOSSIANS 1:19–20

CHRIST ALONE
CAN BRING LASTING PEACE—
PEACE WITH GOD—
PEACE AMONG MEN AND NATIONS—
AND PEACE WITHIN OUR HEARTS.

BILLY GRAHAM

Christ is the Morning Star who,
when the night of this world is past,
brings to His saints the promise of
the light of life and opens everlasting day.

VENERABLE BEDE

Christ had neither money, nor riches, nor earthly kingdom,
for He gave the same to kings and princes. But He reserved
one thing peculiarly to Himself, which no human creature
or angel could do—namely, to conquer sin and death, the
devil and hell, and in the midst of death to deliver and
save those that through His Word believe in Him.

MARTIN LUTHER

When Christ came into the world, peace was sung;
and when He went out of the world,
peace was bequested.

FRANCIS BACON

. . .

PEACE, PERFECT PEACE,
IN THIS DARK WORLD OF SIN?
THE BLOOD OF JESUS
WHISPERS PEACE WITHIN.

W. H. BICKERSTETH

. . .

A great many people are trying to make peace,
but that has already been done.
God has not left it for us to do;
all we have to do is enter into it.

DWIGHT L. MOODY

FATHER,

Thank You for sending Your Son to earth, for His lessons of love and faith, and for shedding the blood of Your Beloved to offer us peace in an often unsettling world. How great is Your love for us, Lord. Help me to remember You every minute of every day, to know You more in my heart, and to share Your love with the world. This Christmas, may we all be reminded of the greatest gift we can receive—a personal relationship with You through Your Son. . .and the faith He bestows in our hearts.

Amen.

BE AT PEACE WITH GOD

"Peace I leave with you; my peace I give you.
I do not give to you as the world gives.
Do not let your hearts be troubled
and do not be afraid."

JOHN 14:27

• • •

"My Presence will go with you,
and I will give you rest."

EXODUS 33:14

• • •

God will never let you be shaken
or moved from your place near His heart.

JONI EARECKSON TADA

I WILL LIE DOWN
AND SLEEP IN PEACE,
FOR YOU ALONE, O LORD,
MAKE ME DWELL IN SAFETY.

PSALM 4:8

. . .

"Submit to God and be at peace with him;

in this way prosperity will come to you."

JOB 22:21

Peace does not mean the end of all our striving,
Joy does not mean the drying of our tears.
Peace is the power that comes to souls arriving
Up to the light where God Himself appears.

G. A. STUDDERT KENNEDY

. . .

IF WE EVER are to attain the true divine peace, and be completely united to God, all that is not absolutely necessary, either bodily or spiritually, must be cast off; everything that could interpose itself to an unlawful extent between us and Him, and lead us astray: For He alone will be Lord in our hearts, and none other; for divine love can admit of no rival.

JOHANNES TAULER

Like a river glorious is God's perfect peace,
Over all victorious in its bright increase;
Perfect, yet it floweth fuller every day,
Perfect, yet it groweth deeper all the way.
Stayed upon Jehovah, hearts are fully blest;
Finding, as He promised, perfect peace and rest.

FRANCES RIDLEY HAVERGAL

WE HAVE PEACE WITH GOD BY THE RIGHTEOUSNESS OF CHRIST, AND PEACE OF CONSCIENCE BY THE FRUITS OF RIGHTEOUSNESS IN OURSELVES.

THOMAS MANTON

WHO except God can give you peace?
Has the world ever been able to satisfy the heart?

ST. GERARD MAJELLA

IT is of great importance that you endeavor, at all times, to keep your hearts in peace; that you may keep pure that temple of God. The way to keep it in peace is to enter into it by means of inward silence. When you see yourself more sharply assaulted, retreat into that region of peace; and you will find a fortress that will enable you to triumph over all your enemies, visible and invisible, and over all their snares and temptations. Within your own soul resides divine and sovereign succor. Retreat within it, and all will be quiet, secure, peaceable, and calm. Thus, by means of mental silence, which can only be attained with divine help, you may look for tranquility in tumult; for solitude in company; for light in darkness; for forgetfulness in pressures; for vigor in despondency; for courage in fear; for resistance in temptation; and for quiet in tribulation.

WILLIAM BACKHOUSE AND JAMES JANSEN

Can anything ever separate us from Christ's love? Does it mean he no longer loves us if we have trouble or calamity, or are persecuted, or are hungry or cold or in danger or threatened with death? No, despite all these things, over-whelming victory is ours through Christ, who loved us. And I am convinced that nothing can ever separate us from his love. Death can't, and life can't. The angels can't, and the demons can't. Our fears for today, our worries about tomorrow, and even the powers of hell can't keep God's love away. . . . Nothing in all creation will ever be able to separate us from the love of God that is revealed in Christ Jesus our Lord.

ROMANS 8:35, 37–39 NLT

GREAT PEACE HAVE THEY WHO LOVE YOUR LAW, AND NOTHING CAN MAKE THEM STUMBLE.

PSALM 119:165

God's peace. . .is far more wonderful than the human mind can understand. His peace will keep your thoughts and your hearts quiet and at rest.

PHILIPPIANS 4:7 TLB

ASK GOD FOR PEACE AND SEE WHAT A TRANSFORMATION WILL TAKE PLACE IN YOUR LIFE.

BILLY GRAHAM

Son, now will I teach you the way of peace and true freedom. (Lord, do as You say; for this is delightful for me to hear.) Study, son, to do the will of another rather than your own. Choose always to have less rather than more. Seek always the lowest place; and to be inferior to everyone. Wish always and pray that the will of God may be wholly fulfilled in you. Behold, such a person enters the land of peace and rest.

THOMAS À KEMPIS

He will give us peace in trouble.

When there is a storm without,

He will make peace within.

The world can create trouble in peace,

but God can create peace in trouble.

THOMAS WATSON

If I alone might have all the solace and comfort of this world, and might use the delights of this world according to my own desire and without sin, it is certain that they would not long endure. And so, my soul cannot be fully comforted or perfectly refreshed, except in God alone, who is the Comforter of the poor in spirit and the Embracer of the humble and low in heart.

THOMAS À KEMPIS

...

IT WILL GREATLY COMFORT YOU IF YOU CAN SEE GOD'S HAND IN BOTH YOUR LOSSES AND YOUR CROSSES.

CHARLES HADDON SPURGEON

FATHER,

I sometimes try to comfort myself with the ways of the world, to create my own peace through a false security. I often forget that the only true peace and security I will ever know comes from You. Your grace and forgiveness I sometimes take for granted, yet they are the most wonderful gifts a Father can give. Through You I am able to breathe freely, to let my heart rest in knowing that my life is in Your hands, and to be at peace. Thank You, Lord, for these precious gifts. They are undeserved, unsolicited, and often misunderstood. But I know that You love me, Lord, and You provide for me. I see evidence of this every minute of every day. My soul is at peace in Your love. Thank You for blessing me.

Amen.

FINDING PEACE AT CHRISTMASTIME

Amidst the hustle and bustle,
remember the reason for the season,
the Christ child who was sent to earth to save us all. . . .

. . .

When we celebrate Christmas we are celebrating
that amazing time when the Word that shouted
all the galaxies into being, limited all power, and
for the love of us came to us in the powerless
body of a human baby.

MADELINE L'ENGLE

. . .

When anxiety was great within me,
your consolation brought joy to my soul.

PSALM 94:19

*Let your spirit be blessed by the grace
our Lord grants and the joy He refreshes.
Take a deep breath and experience
the wonder of His blessings!*

Christ is not only a remedy for your
weariness and trouble, but He will give you an
abundance of the contrary, joy and delight.

JONATHAN EDWARDS

AMID THE DARKNESS OF SIN, THE LIGHT OF GOD'S GRACE SHINES IN.

AUTHOR UNKNOWN

Where the will of God leads you,
the grace of God will keep you.

AUTHOR UNKNOWN

. . .

GRACE IS
THE GIFT OF CHRIST,
WHO EXPOSES THE GULF
WHICH SEPARATES
GOD AND MAN,
AND, BY EXPOSING IT,
BRIDGES IT.

KARL BARTH

*Do you remember
how to see Christmas
through the eyes of a child?*

It's good to be children sometimes, and never better than at Christmas, when its mighty Founder was a child Himself.

CHARLES DICKENS

People were bringing little children to him [Jesus] in order that he might touch them; and the disciples spoke sternly to them. But when Jesus saw this, he was indignant and said to them, "Let the little children come to me; do not stop them; for it is to such as these that the kingdom of God belongs. Truly I tell you, whoever does not receive the kingdom of God as a little child will never enter it." And he took them up in his arms, laid his hands on them, and blessed them.

MARK 10:13–16 NRSV

Try to remember when you were a child. . .when, in the days of tradition and togetherness, Christmas was the most exciting time of year. You were the first one awake on Christmas morning, unable to control your enthusiasm, running down the stairs to see what gifts were left for you under the tree. Did you get that toy you most wanted? Was there a wrapped package the size of the gift you were hoping for? Surely it was there somewhere. . .and you fought your way through a mountain of gifts, knowing in your heart that your parents had taken care of you, trusting that they had provided.

Now ask yourself, do you have the same kind of excitement in your heart today? Do you still have the same faith? God provides for us, not only on Christmas day, but every day. He gives us everything we need, including gifts that we don't even realize we need. We trust that He knows our hearts and loves us, and that He will give us peace through our relationship with Him. Every day we receive His grace, His love, the security of knowing that He has better things in store. This Christmas, receive these gifts as a child would receive a new toy—with excitement, thanks, and, most of all, a joyful heart!

When you were a child, you may or may not have believed in Santa Claus. But you made a list of what you wanted for Christmas and somehow managed to get it to the person who could make your dreams come true. This Christmas, try a new exercise. Ask the One who can answer your prayers for the desires of your heart.

The following is a suggested list—a "spiritual" wish list. But ask God for what is on your heart at this moment.

Lord, remind me that this season is all about Your Son and how

He died for my sins so that I may be with You for eternity.

Help me to not get bogged down with the things that society

says about Christmas, for I know that Christmas was made

for one reason—to celebrate Your Son.

Let me show my family the kind of love and grace

that You have shown me.

Allow me to be a beacon of light, shining for You

even through the darkness of winter.

Let this world find peace in knowing that You are in control,

and that Your desire is for us to love one another.

Ask God for what you want and experience the peace He gives you.
Breathe. Love. Rejoice.

FATHER,

Sometimes I find myself feeling rather *un*-joyful during the Christmas season. I know I should be celebrating the birth of the Messiah, the one true God. I should be praising Him in everything I do, sharing His love with others, and doing good deeds to show my love for Him. Yet I find myself frustrated—waiting in lines, searching endlessly for the proper gift, reluctantly forcing myself to dish out batch after batch of snowman cookies, and worrying about finances. Please help me to focus on You—the reason for the season. For You are the hope in my heart, the love in my life, and the skip in my step. Help me to slow down and take time for myself, so that I may appreciate all of Your creation, and so my heart can be at rest in relinquishing my control to You.

Amen.

SHARE HIS JOY

Joy is peace dancing;
peace is joy resting.

AUTHOR UNKNOWN

Seek joy in what you give,
not in what you get.

AUTHOR UNKNOWN

To be simply ensconced in God
is true joy.

C. C. COLTON

THE WHOLE POINT OF THE LETTER TO THE PHILIPPIANS IS: I DO REJOICE— DO YOU REJOICE?

BENGEL

Desire joy and thank God for it.
Renounce it, if need be, for other's sake.
That's joy beyond joy.

ROBERT BROWNING

J	JESUS
O	OTHERS
Y	YOURSELF

If you use the joy rule and think of Jesus,

then others, then yourself,

you will really feel true joy.

AUTHOR UNKNOWN

There is not one blade of grass,

there is no color in this world that

is not intended to make us rejoice.

JOHN CALVIN

Real joy comes not from ease or riches from praise of men, but from doing something worthwhile.

SIR WILFRED GRENFELL

. . .

Join the great company of those who make the barren places of life fruitful with kindness. Carry a vision of heaven in your hearts, and you shall make your name, your college, the world, correspond to that vision. Your success and happiness lie within you. External conditions are the accidents of life, its outer wrappings. The great, enduring realities are love and service. Joy is the holy fire that keeps our purpose warm and our intelligence aglow. Resolve to keep happy, and your joy and you shall form an invincible host against difficulty.

HELEN KELLER

JOY IS THE EXPERIENCE OF KNOWING THAT YOU ARE UNCONDITIONALLY LOVED.

HENRI NOUWEN

Joy is the wine that God is ever pouring

Into the hearts of those who strive with Him,

Lighting their eye to vision and airing,

Strengthening their arms to warfare glad and grim.

G. A. STUDDERT KENNEDY

Rejoicing is clearly a spiritual
command. To ignore it is disobedience.

CHARLES SWINDOLL

...

ONE FILLED WITH JOY
PREACHES WITHOUT PREACHING.

MOTHER TERESA

...

The opposite of joy is not sorrow.
It is unbelief.

LESLIE WEATHERHEAD

The religion of Christ is the religion of joy. Christ came to take away our sins, to roll off our curse, to unbind our chains, to open our prison house, to cancel our debt; in a word, to give us the oil of joy for mourning, the garment of praise for the spirit of heaviness. Is not this joy? Where can we find a joy so real, so deep, so pure, so lasting? There is every element of joy— deep, ecstatic, satisfying, sanctifying joy—in the gospel of Christ. The believer in Jesus is essentially a happy man. The child of God is, from necessity, a joyful man. His sins are forgiven, his soul is justified, his person is adopted, his trials are blessings, his conflicts are victories, his death is immortality, his future is a heaven of inconceivable, unthought of, untold, and endless blessedness. With such a God, such a Savior, and such a hope, is he not, ought he not, to be a joyful man?

OCTAVIUS WINSLOW

JOY TO THE WORLD

Joy to the world, the Lord is come!
Let earth receive her King;
Let every heart prepare Him room,
And heaven and nature sing,
And heaven and nature sing,
And heaven, and heaven, and nature sing.

Joy to the world, the Savior reigns!
Let men their songs employ;
While fields and floods, rocks, hills and plains
Repeat the sounding joy,
Repeat the sounding joy,
Repeat, repeat, the sounding joy.

No more let sins and sorrows grow,
Nor thorns infest the ground;
He comes to make His blessings flow
Far as the curse is found,
Far as the curse is found,
Far as, far as, the curse is found.

He rules the world with truth and grace,
And makes the nations prove
The glories of His righteousness,
And wonders of His love,
And wonders of His love,
And wonders, wonders, of His love.

ISAAC WATTS

LET THERE BE
PEACE ON EARTH

But peace does not rest in the charters and covenants alone. It lies in the hearts and minds of all people. So let us not rest all our hopes on parchment and on paper. . . . Let us strive to build peace, a desire for peace, a willingness to work for peace in the hearts and minds of all of our people. I believe that we can. I believe the problems of human destiny are not beyond the reach of human beings.

JOHN F. KENNEDY

WE SHALL FIND PEACE.
WE SHALL HEAR THE ANGELS,
WE SHALL SEE THE SKY
SPARKLING WITH DIAMONDS.

ANTON CHECKHOV

FIRST KEEP THE PEACE WITHIN YOURSELF, THEN YOU CAN ALSO BRING PEACE TO OTHERS.

THOMAS À KEMPIS

. . .

I like to believe that people in the long run are going to do more to promote peace than our governments. Indeed, I think that people want peace so much that one of these days governments had better get out of the way and let them have it.

DWIGHT D. EISENHOWER

SO LONG AS WE LIVE
AMONG MEN,
LET US CHERISH HUMANITY.

ANDRE GIDE

. . .

We look forward to the time when the power

to love will replace the love of power. Then will our world

know the blessings of peace.

WILLIAM GLADSTONE

. . .

A HARVEST OF PEACE
IS PRODUCED FROM
A SEED OF CONTENTMENT.

INDIAN PROVERB

Lord, make me an instrument of thy peace.
Where there is hatred, let me sow love;
Where there is injury, pardon;
Where there is doubt, faith;
Where there is despair, hope;
Where there is darkness, light;
Where there is sadness, joy.
O Divine Master, grant that I may not so much seek
To be consoled as to console;
Not so much to be understood as to understand;
Not so much to be loved as to love;
For it is in giving that we receive;
It is in pardoning that we are pardoned;
It is in dying that we are born to the eternal life.

ATTRIBUTED TO ST. FRANCIS OF ASSISI

. . .

Peace cannot be achieved through violence,
it can only be attained through understanding.

RALPH WALDO EMERSON

. . .

Keep your heart in peace; let nothing
in this world disturb it; everything has an end.

JOHN OF THE CROSS

PEACE REIGNS WHERE OUR LORD REIGNS.

JULIAN OF NORWICH

Your life and my life flow into each other as wave flows into wave, and unless there is peace and joy and freedom for you, there can be no real peace or joy or freedom for me. To see reality—not as we expect it to be but as it is—is to see that unless we live for each other and in and through each other, we do not really live very satisfactorily; that there can really be life only where there really is, in just this sense, love.

FREDERICK BUECHNER, *The Magnificent Defeat*

THE LORD GIVES STRENGTH TO HIS PEOPLE; THE LORD BLESSES HIS PEOPLE WITH PEACE.

PSALM 29:11

It isn't enough to talk about peace.
One must believe in it.
And it isn't enough to believe in it.
One must work at it.

ELEANOR ROOSEVELT

...

FATHER,

Sometimes I feel that, with the turmoil in this world, a chance for peace seems unattainable. I try to live in my own little world and distance myself from the darkness, but I can only distance myself for so long. I have to believe that one person can make a difference, Lord. And I know how I can be that person. I will tell people of Your love. If I can share the gifts You've given me with just one person, over time, thousands could be affected for Your glory. The more people who have Your love in their hearts, the more who will know true peace. This Christmas, make me a messenger. Let me shout Your name from the hilltops! Let me show others what good Your Word has done in my life. May I carry Your peace with me always, Lord, and may I make a difference in this world—for You. In Thy name, I pray with all of my heart.

Amen.